ARTphabet

An Early Education Guide to Process-Focused Art from A to Z

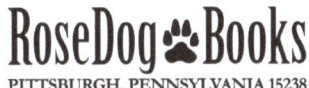

RoseDog Books
PITTSBURGH, PENNSYLVANIA 15238

RoseDog Books
585 Alpha Drive
Suite 103
Pittsburgh, PA 15238
Visit our website at *www.rosedogbookstore.com*

ISBN: 978-1-6461-0330-0
eISBN: 978-1-6464-0284-6

Let us explore ways to reinforce letter sounds through developmentally appropriate art experiences. These art applications are process-focused as opposed to product-focused. Rather than following instructions toward an intended product, *ART-*phabet focuses on the process, encouraging children's individuality and creativity from A to Z.

*There are no step-by-step instructions in process-focused art. Nor is there a right or wrong way to create. This allows the art experience to be calming. The art is the children's own, original and unique.

*In product-focused art children must follow instructions. There is a right and a wrong way to proceed toward a finished product. Children often strive to duplicate an adult's example as opposed to using their imagination and displaying creativity.

*Resource: NAEYC publication

There is no wrong way to make process-focused art.
Get creative! Having fun is the most important part!

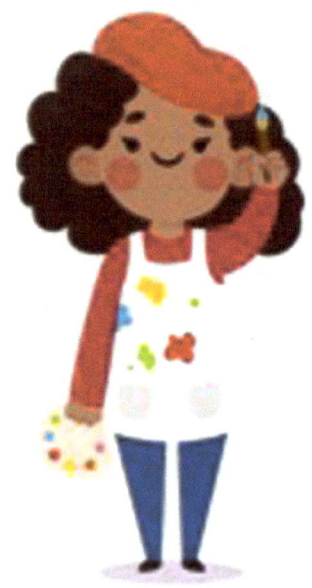

Creative art can support children in all areas of development.

Physical Development

Art activities support children's large and small muscle development, as well as their eye-hand coordination. Using crayons, markers, and paint-brushes helps children practice the fine motor control they will need for writing.

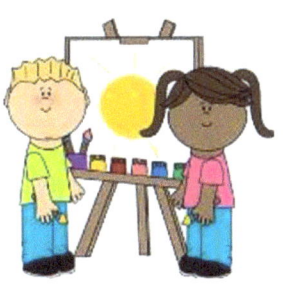

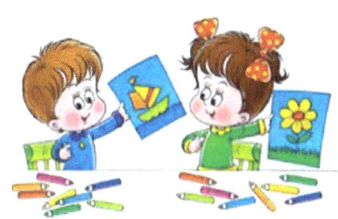

Social Development

Working together in the art area, children learn to share, to interact with others, to be responsible for cleanup and to put materials away. These are positive and important changes for social learning.

Cognitive Development

Children can learn names of colors and shapes through creative art activities. They find out what happens when they mix two primary colors to-gether and get a secondary color. Giving chil-dren opportunities to carefully examine and study objects of nature and then asking them to draw what they've seen helps them develop observational skills needed for science.

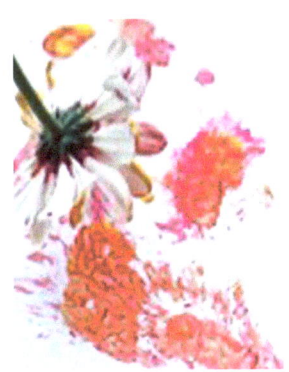

Emotional Development

Through creative art, children may be able to represent experiences that they cannot verbalize. They may draw pictures out of proportion, exaggerating things that are important to them. When we value children's creativity, we help raise their confidence.

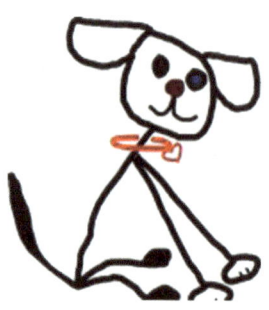

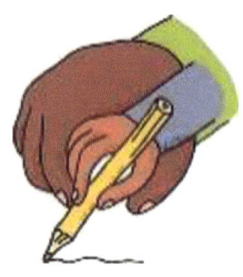

Language and Literacy

Children may illustrate their interpretation of a story or poem. They also may choose to discuss their art and add print to it (on their own or by dictating to an adult).

Developmental Benefits of Creative Art

Fine Motor Skills   Anxiety Relief

Emotional Expression

Sense of Accomplishment

Gross Motor Skills   Tactile Discoveries

Hand-Eye Coordination   Imagination

Extension of Academic Concepts

Focus/Concentration   Experimentation

Symbolic Communication

ARTphabet

A is for ABSTRACTS

Abstracts are a relationship of form and colors as opposed to a recognizable image.

Supply an assortment of rulers and geometric shapes from which children can randomly trace overlaying patterns. Encourage them to color in parts of design.

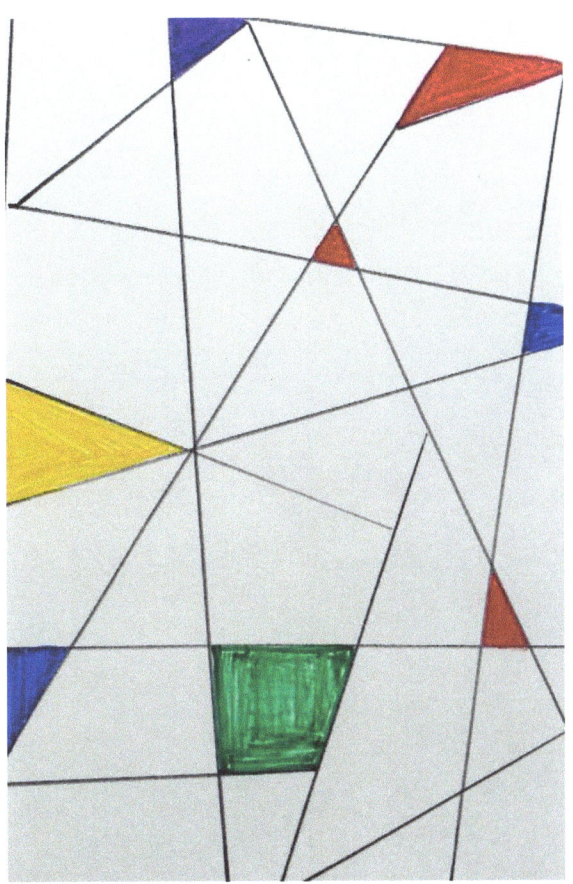

B is for BRAIDING

Cut strips of fabric one inch wide to make braiding manage-
able for little fingers. Secure pieces at the top with a clip.

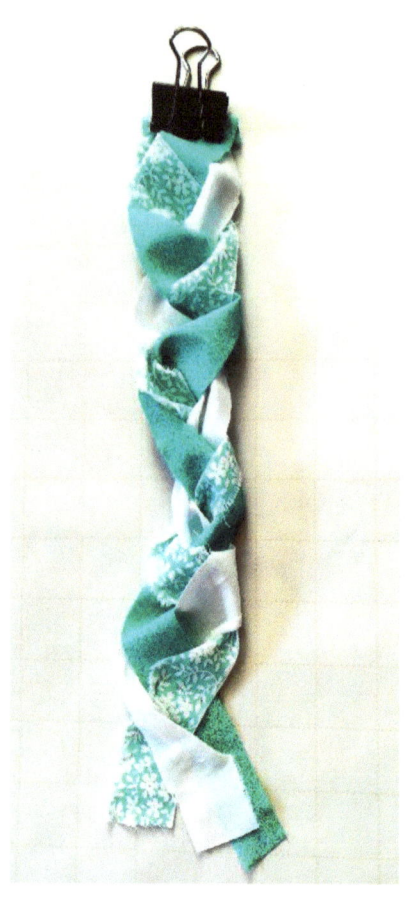

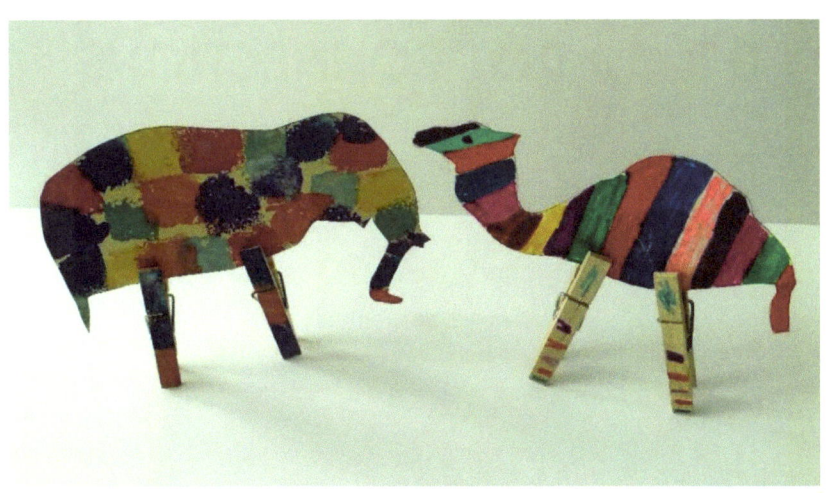

C is for **CLOTHESPIN CREATURES**

Provide clothespins and animal or random card stock shapes.
Children can use crayons or markers to color everything and
attach clothespin legs.

D is for DOT CONNECTIONS

Supply dotted paper and crayons.

Ask the children to connect the dots to form random shapes, designs and letters.

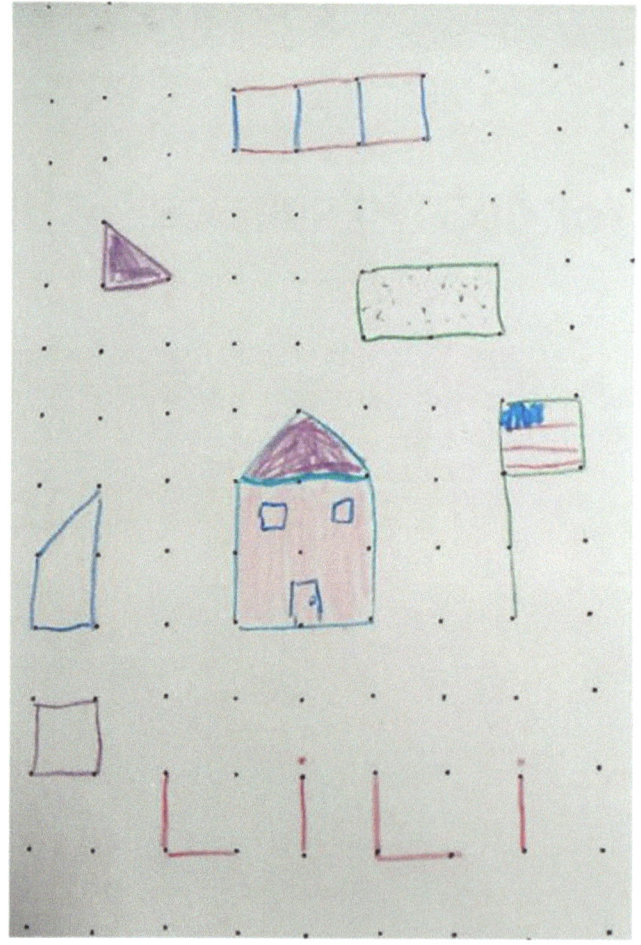

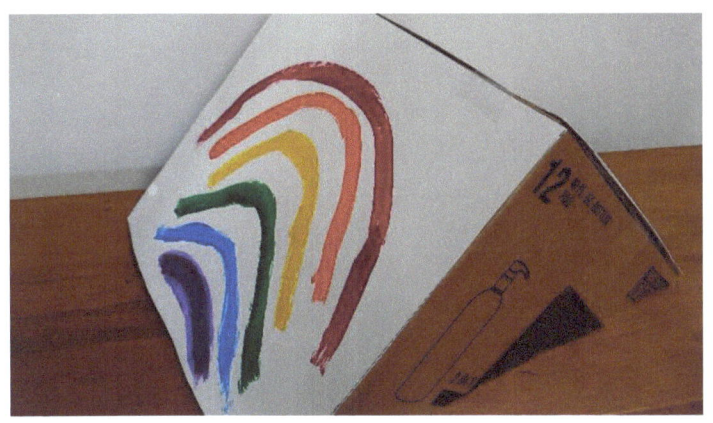

E is for EASEL DOES IT!

The ultimate open-ended art activity!

No easel? No problem! Cut a square carton diagonally for a double-sided table-top easel.

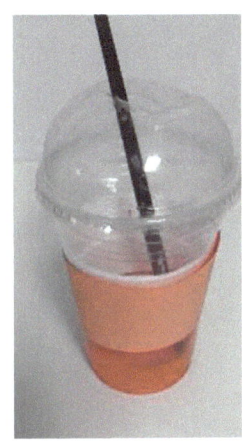

Domed drink cups hold easel paints and brushes.

F is for FINGERPAINT TRANSFER

After children finger paint on a table or cookie sheet, cover their work with plain paper and press down to transfer design.

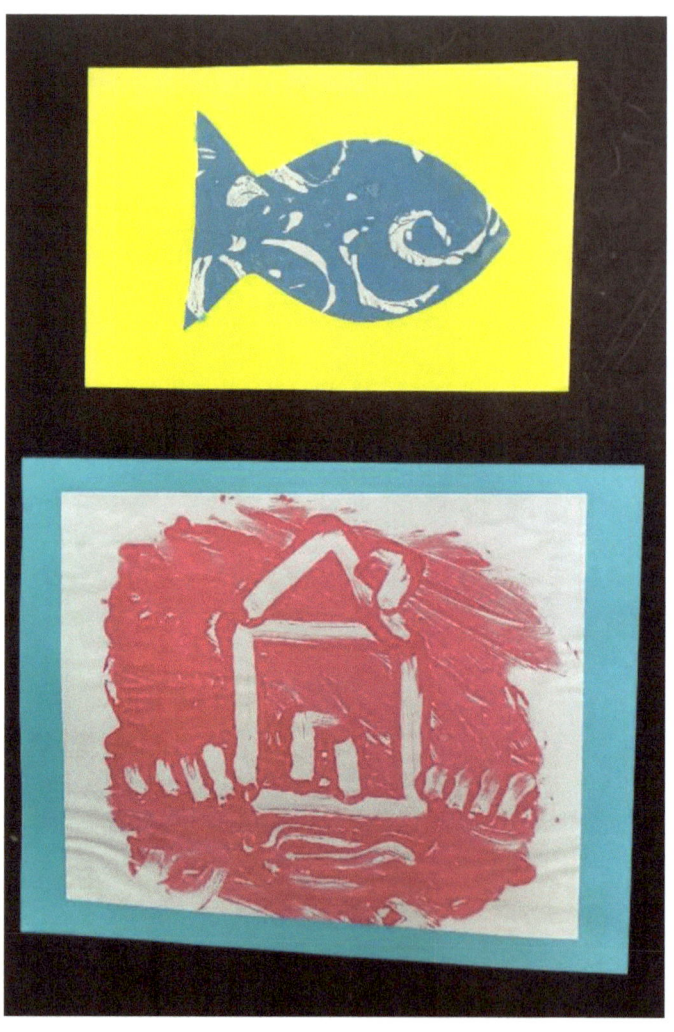

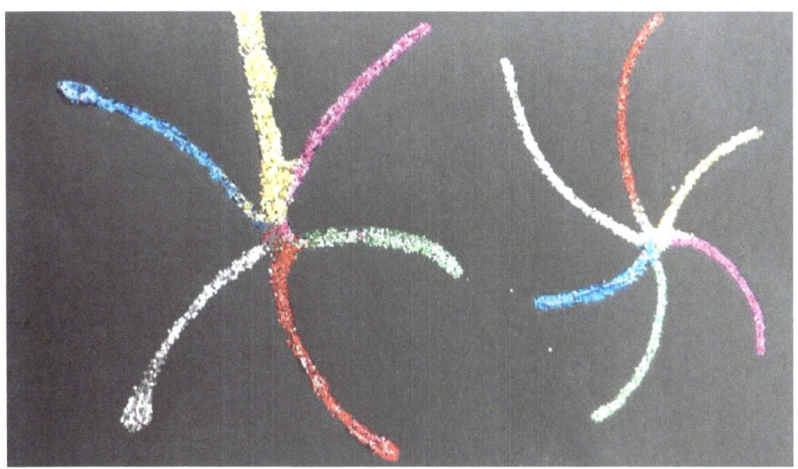

G is for Glue & Glitter Creations

Draw designs using squeeze bottles of glue then sprinkle
with multi-colored glitter.

H is for Hand Tracing

Trace children's hands and lower arms in various positions. Offer crayons and craft materials for the children to create pictures from the tracings.

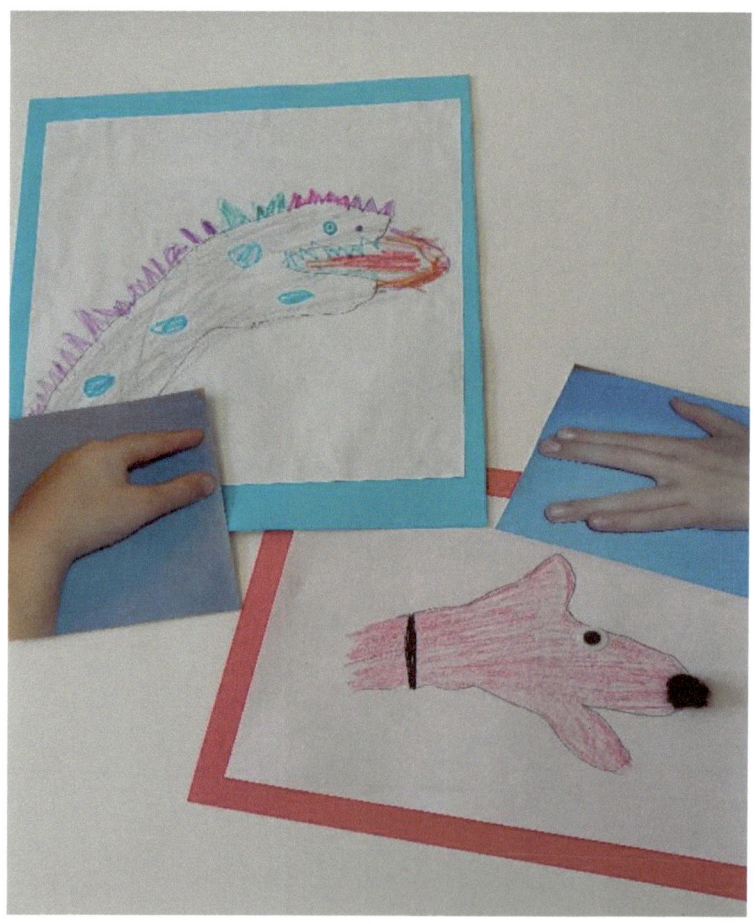

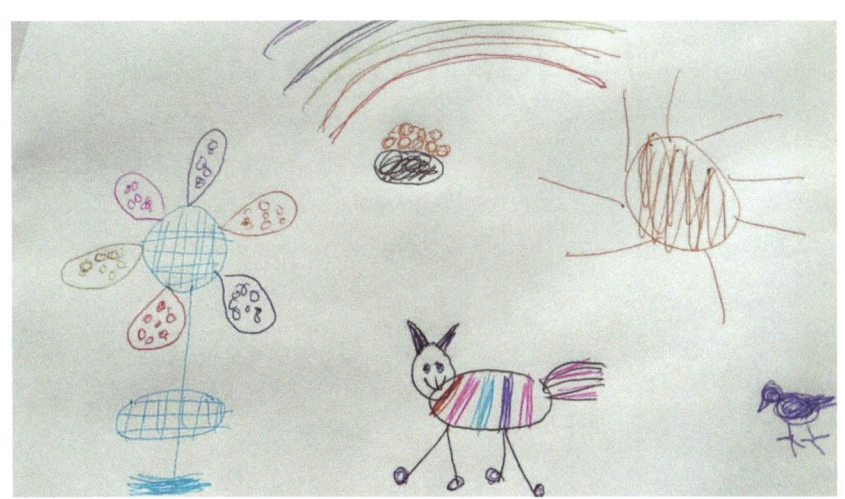

I is for INK DRAWING

Provide pens with various ink colors. Children often pay more attention to detail when using the fine tips of pens.

Some ink is not washable. Close supervision recommended.

J is for JUNK ART

Everybody has a junk drawer! Ask families to donate safe items.
Use non-toxic craft glue and adhere items to sturdy cardboard.

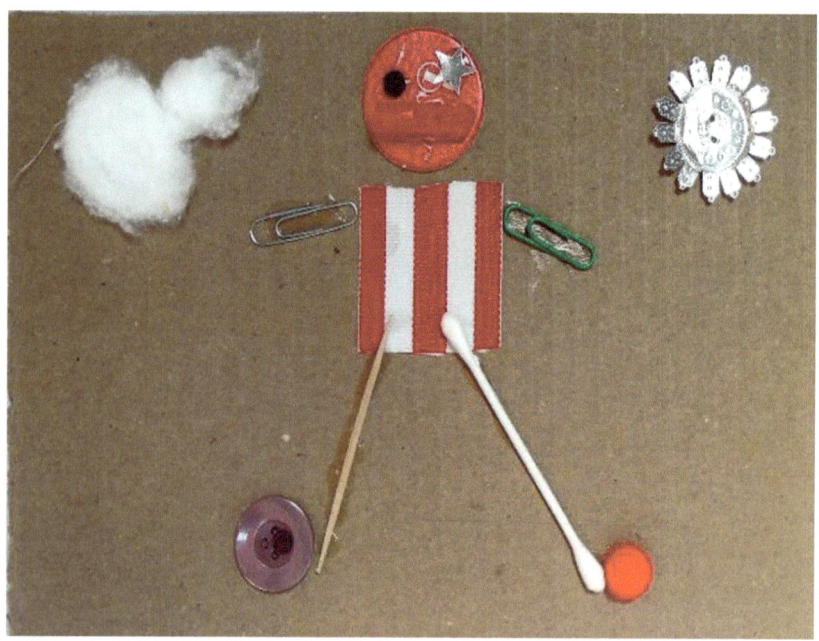

K is for KETCHUP DRAWING

A squeeze bottle of ketchup, a paper
plate and imagination are all that are
needed for this fun activity!

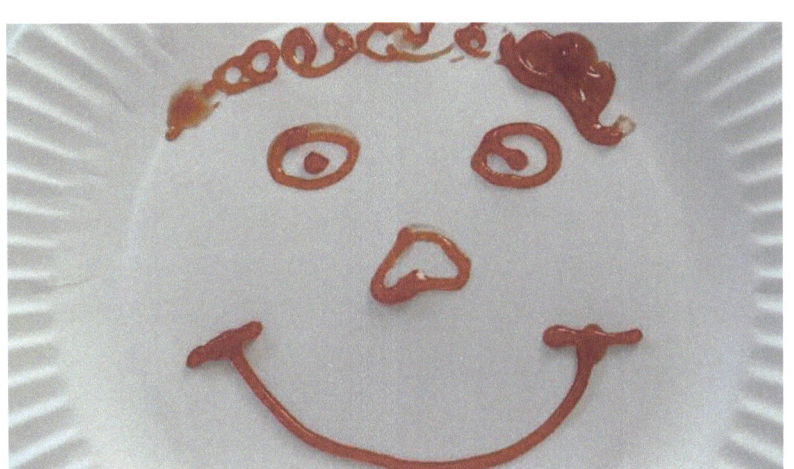

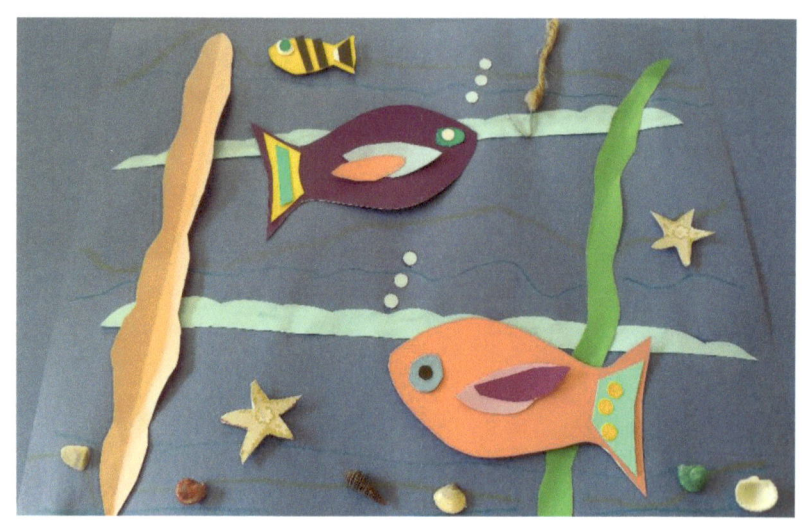

L is for Layering

Start with a crayon colored background. Add depth and dimension by layering varied materials.

M is for MARBLE PARTNER PAINTING

Cut a piece of paper to fit snugly inside a coffee can. Drop marbles into paint and place in can. Secure lid. Children take turns rolling the can back and forth to each other.

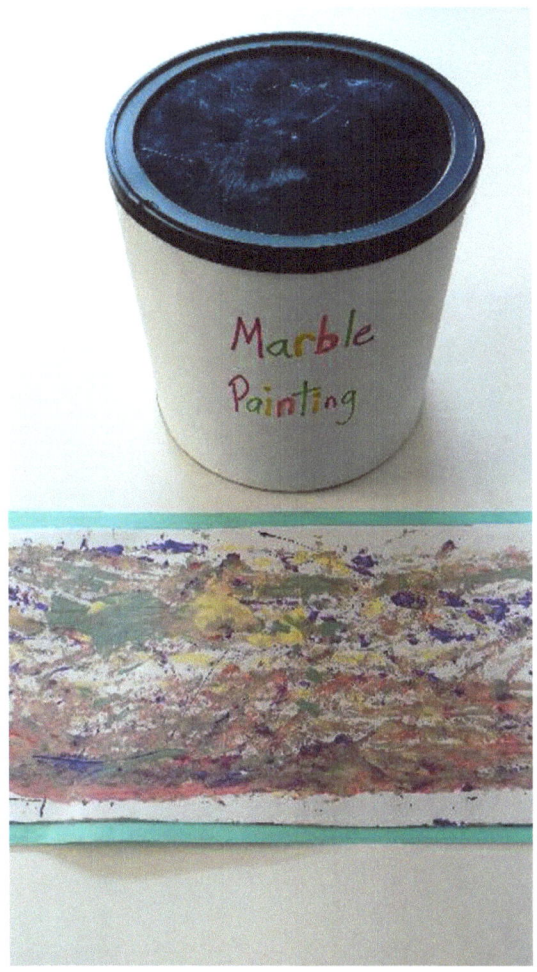

N is for NEWSPAPER NUMBERS

Provide newspapers from which children can cut out numbers. Use the numbers to form random pictures.

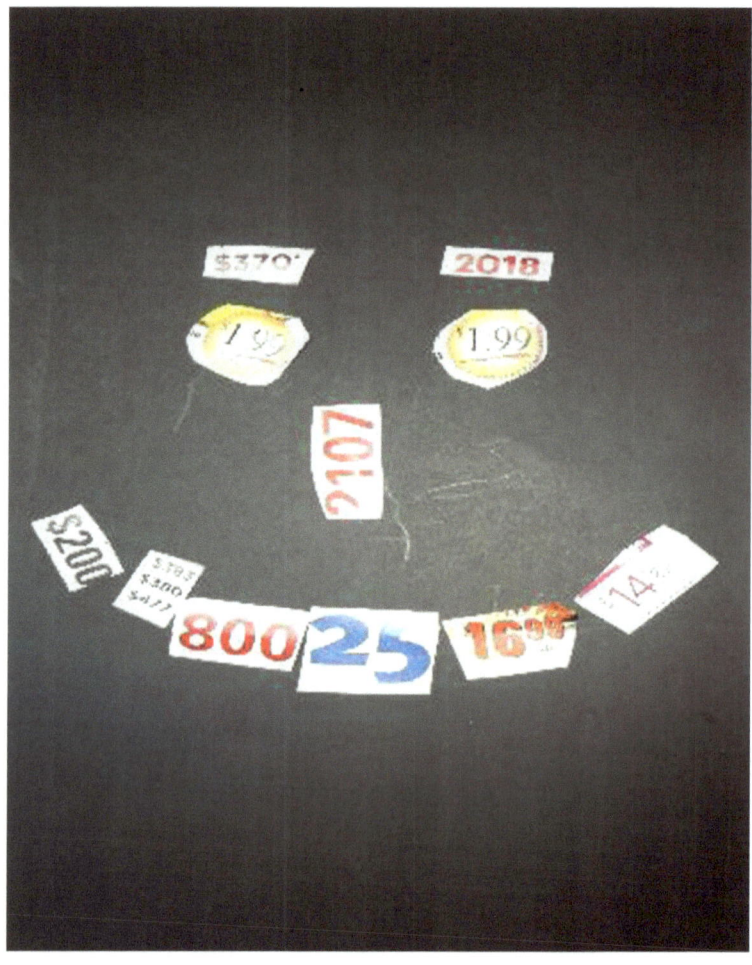

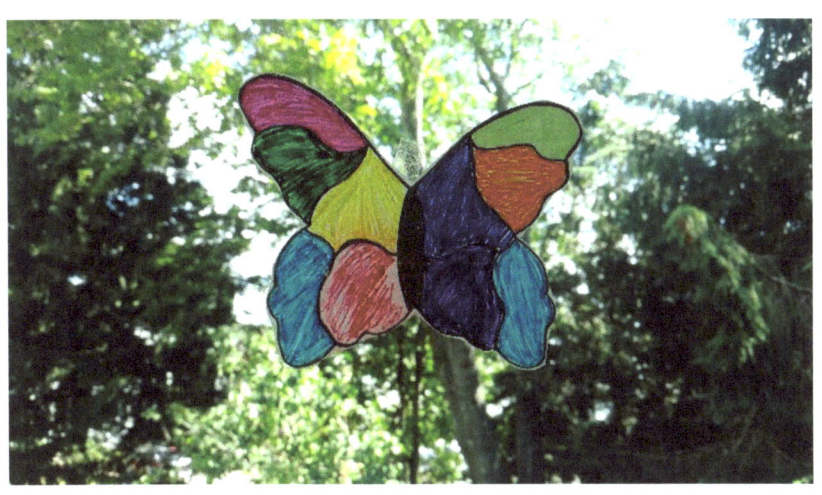

O is for OIL BACKED COLORING

Draw a segmented design defined by black marker. Supply markers in various colors for the children to color in each segment. Dip a small paintbrush in cooking oil and brush on the back of entire drawing. Blot dry. The translucent result looks great on a window!

P is for PAINT CHIP CREATIONS

Ask paint stores to donate paint chips of discontinued colors
to make unique, creative designs.

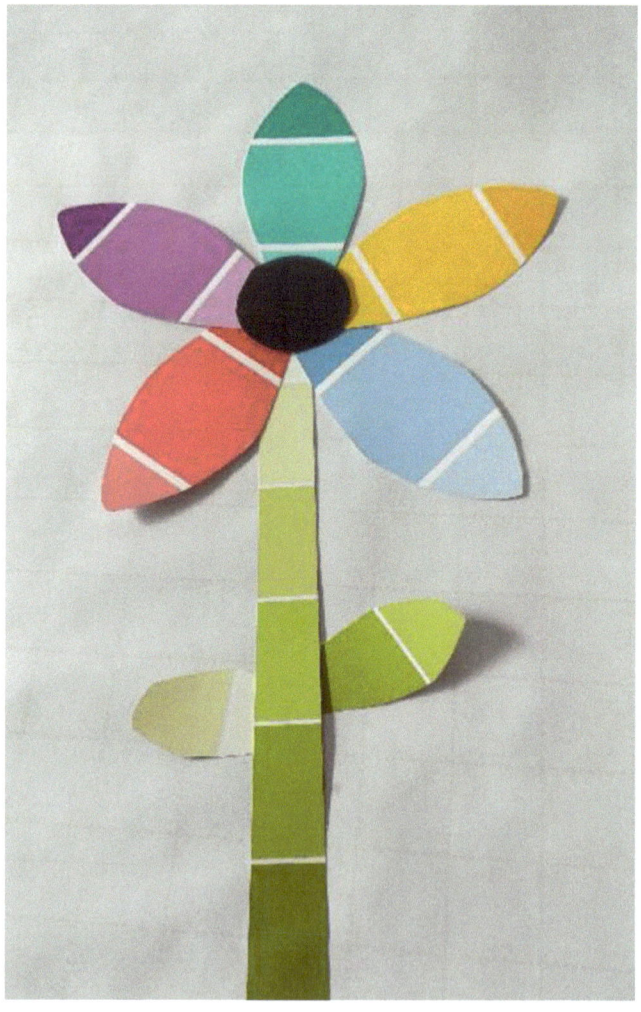

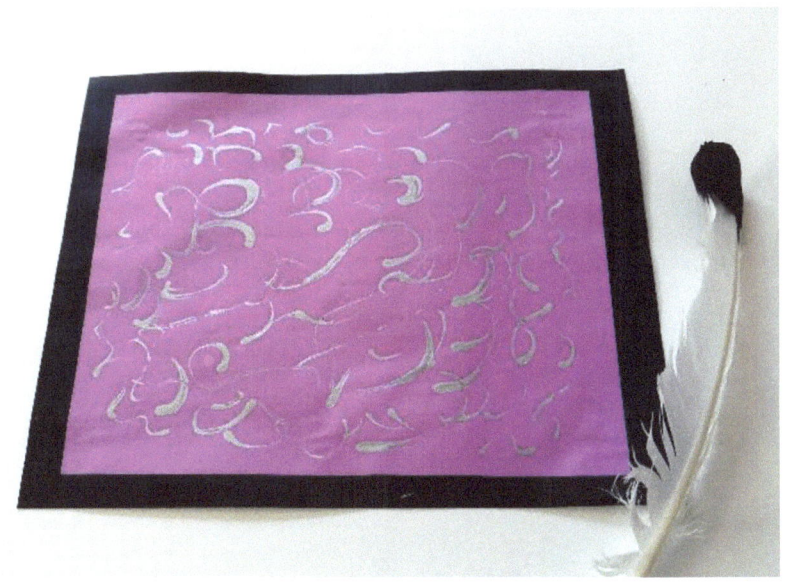

Q is for QUILL WRITING

Explain that people dipped the core of a feather, called a quill, in ink and used it for writing a long time ago. Watered down tempera paint works best for this activity.

R is for ROCK RELIEF

A relief is a projection of forms from a flat background. Make
a heavy collage paste (equal parts flour and salt and enough
water to hold it together). Mix in a few drops of food color-
ing. Spread in deep dish and add rocks of various size and
color. It will harden as it dries.

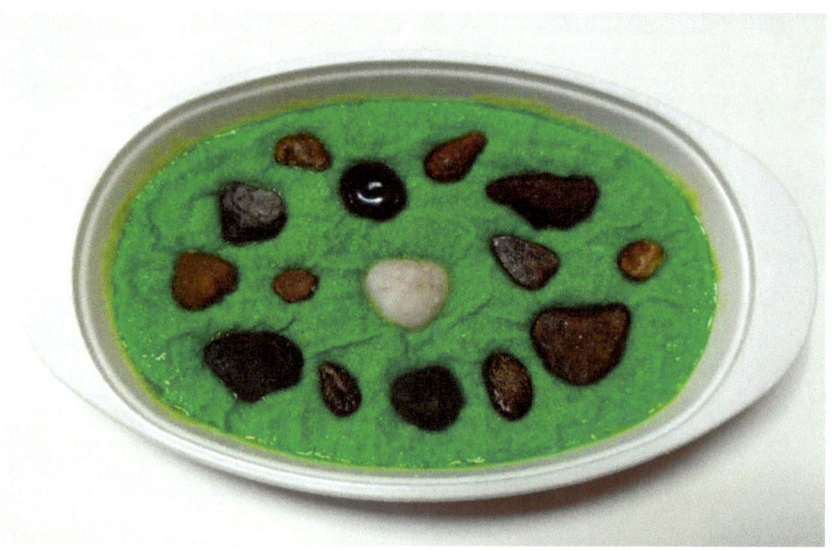

S is for SAND SPRINKLING

Provide containers of colored sand. Have children peel off backing from sticky paper (works better than glue!) and use fingers in a pincher grip to sprinkle on the sand in random designs.

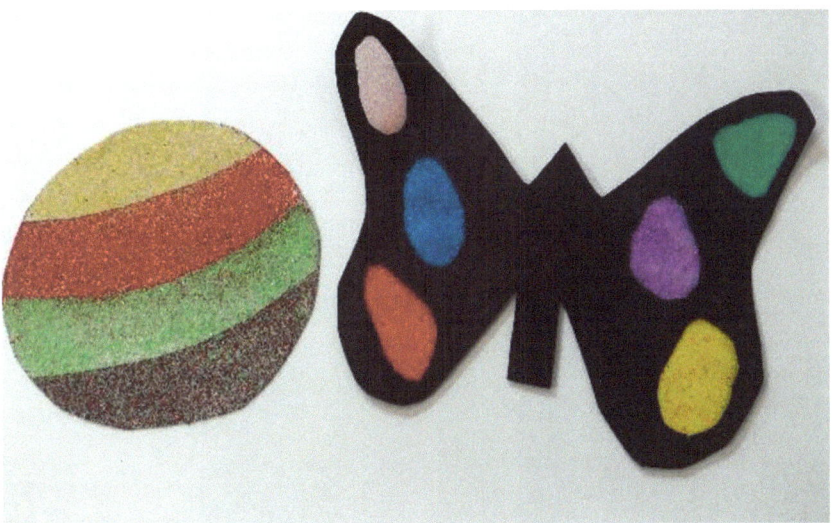

T is for TEXTURAL ARRANGEMENT

Supply an assortment of shapes in various textures. Children arrange the pieces to their liking in this tactile activity.

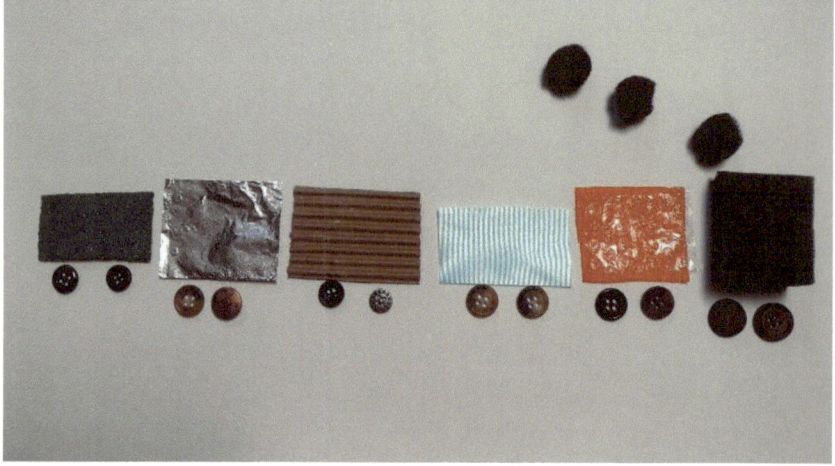

U is for UNDER THE TABLE ART

Attach butcher paper under a table. Provide crayons
and let children lie on their backs to draw under the
table for a unique perspective.

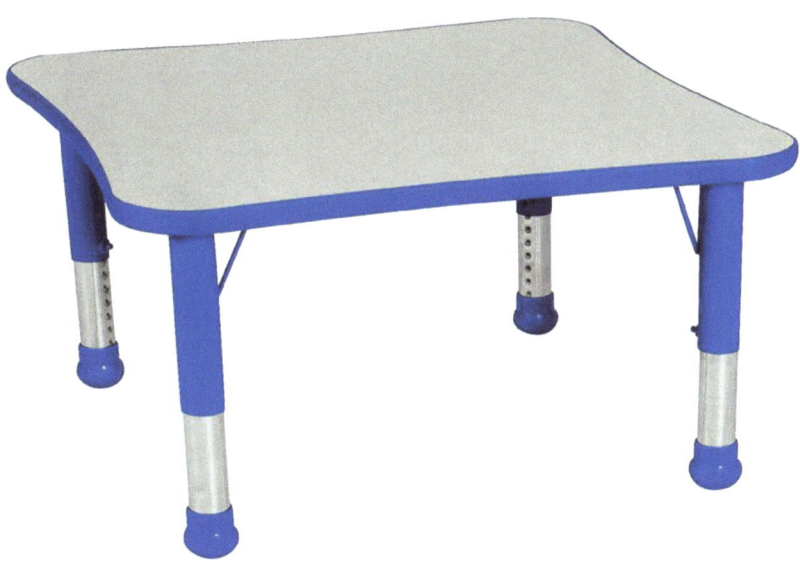

V is for VARIATION OF COLOR

Paint a section of paper with a dark primary color. Add a
drop of white paint to the primary and paint another section.
Repeat until the last section is just a hint of the original color.

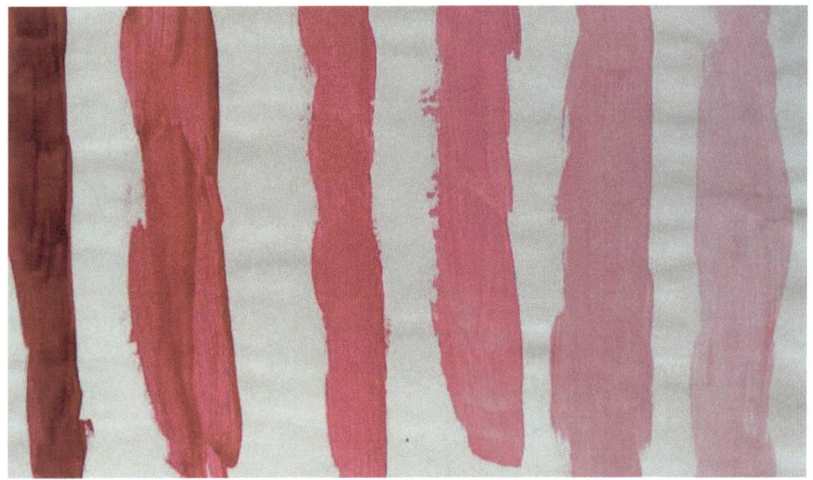

W is for WOOD CRAFT

Provide smooth, sanded pieces of wood and a large assortment of hardware items. Using non-toxic wood glue, adhere the items to the wood, forming free style designs.

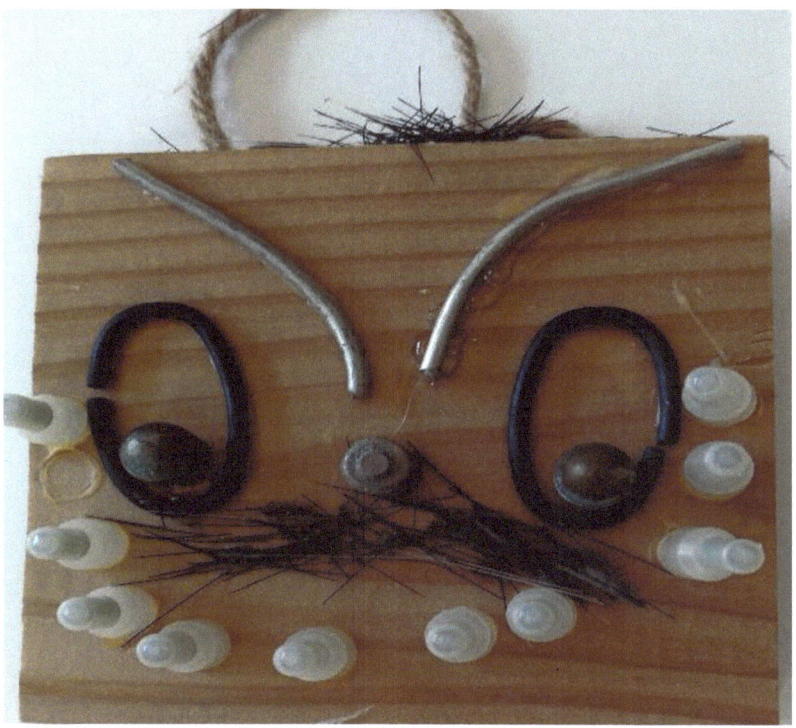

X is for X MARKS THE SPOT

Children can explore patterns and textures as they cut strips of scrapbooking paper and form into the letter **X** multiple times.

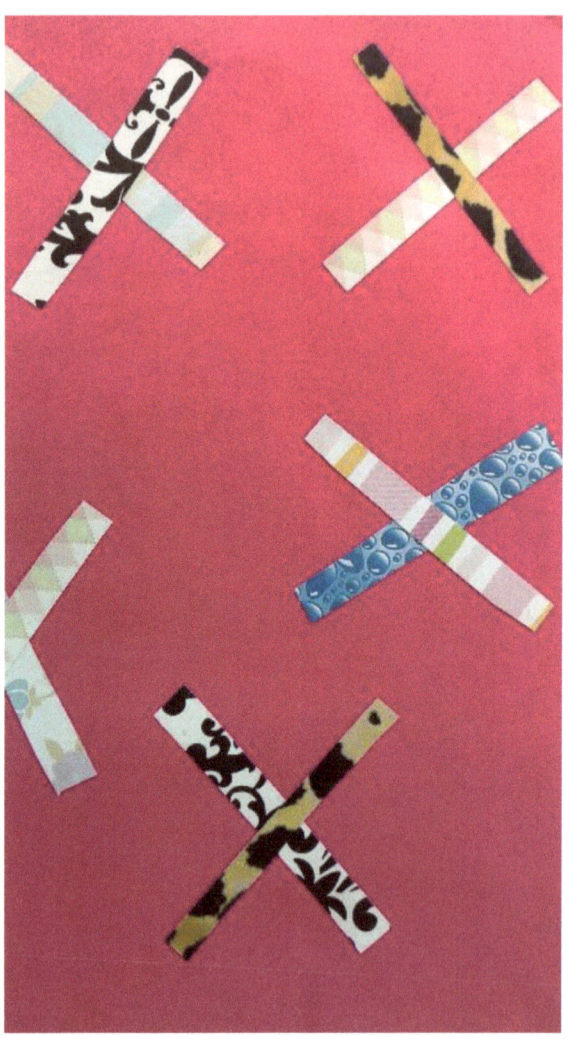

Y is for YARN DESIGNS

Holding by clothespins, dip strands of yarn into glue diluted
with water. Arrange onto cardstock and let dry.

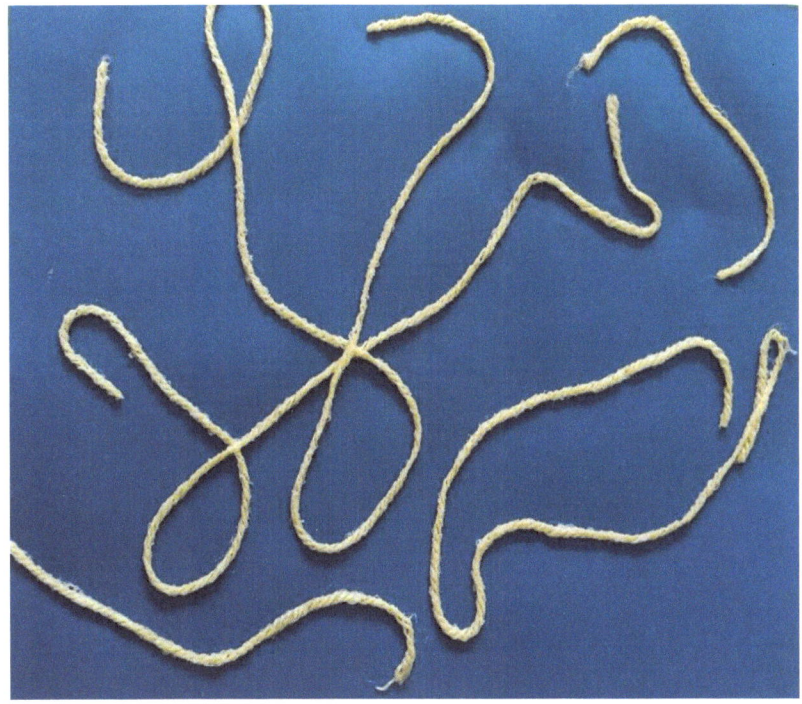

Z is for ZIPPER BAG CREATIONS

Cut paper to fit inside a gallon sized zippered storage bag. Add paints and seal bag (you may want to tape it also as a precaution). Let children squeeze and squish the bag until the paper is fully covered with paint. Suggest they draw the letter Z with their finger on the outside of the bag. Remove the paper and let dry.

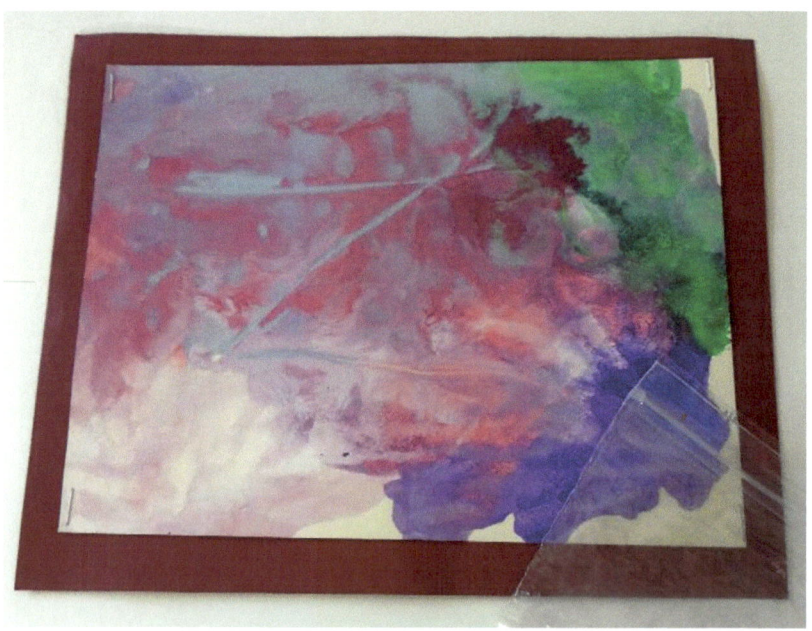

www.ingramcontent.com/pod-product-compliance
Lightning Source LLC
Chambersburg PA
CBHW041116180526
45172CB00001B/279